Contents

1 Key features of Abacus 2
  The Abacus programme 2

2 The National Numeracy Strategy 3
  The National Context 3
  The three-part lesson 4

3 Classroom management 5
  The Teacher Card 5
  Classroom organisation 5
  Organising groups 5

4 The Abacus materials 6
  Mental Warm-up Activities 6
  Teacher Cards 6
  Activity Book 8
  Textbooks 8
  Photocopy Masters 9
  Resource Bank and Games Pack 9
  Simmering Activities 9
  Homework Book 10
  Assessment Book 10
  Challenge Book 11
  Numeracy Support Book 11

5 An Abacus Unit 12
  Supporting teachers in teaching and
    children in learning 13
  Flexibility in the teaching of each topic 14
  Flexibility in classroom management 14
  Teaching in mixed-age classes 14
  Starting the lesson 15
  Main teaching activity 15
  The plenary session 17
  Homework 18
  Assessment 19

6 Differentiation 20
  Whole class focus 20
  Keeping the children together 20
  Special needs 21

7 Teaching strategies 22
  Questioning 23

8 Specific guidance on
  mathematical content 25
  Introducing Abacus 25
  Place-value 26
  Addition and subtraction 26
  Multiplication and division 27
  Money 27
  Measures 28
  Weight and mass 28
  Area and perimeter 28
  Shapes 28
  Polygons and polyhedra 28
  Angle 29
  Position 29
  Graphs 29
  Probability 29

9 Framework for teaching
  mathematics matching chart 30

10 Classroom materials 34
  Materials provided in the Resource Bank 34
  Games Pack 34
  Assumed mathematical materials
    in the classroom 34
  Other materials 34

11 Assessment grid (Key Stage 2) 35
  Using and applying mathematics 36
  Number 37
  Shape, Space and Measures 38
  Handling Data 39

12 Planning 40
  Long term planning 40
  Medium term planning 40
  Short term planning 41
  Summary 42
  Planning grids 42
  Exemplar planning grid: autumn 43
  Exemplar planning grid: spring 45
  Exemplar planning grid: summer 47

1 Key features of Abacus

The Abacus programme

Abacus follows the detailed plan of teaching objectives outlined in the Framework for Teaching Mathematics. Furthermore, Abacus, from its inception, has been designed and written with precisely the same approach to the teaching of mathematics as that of the National Numeracy Strategy. Abacus is based on three principles:

Direct and interactive teaching is at the heart of the process of helping children learn mathematics. Children often do not 'discover' strategies; they have to be taught them.

Many mathematical skills and facts, particularly those which help children become fluent in mental calculations, need to be taught clearly, and then rehearsed regularly on a 'little-and-often' basis.

Materials need to support teachers in their teaching, and to help keep classroom management simple and effective. It is not necessary, nor is it desirable, for every classroom teacher to 'reinvent the wheel'. A clear structure of key objectives (with sufficient flexibility for important professional decisions to be left to each teacher in their own specific context) will minimise the hours spent planning and preparing, and maximise the teacher's effectiveness in the classroom.

As well as being based on the same philosophy, Abacus shares several assumptions with the National Numeracy Strategy.
- There will be a daily mathematics lesson.
- The lesson will have a three-part structure. Although the timing will be flexible, and will vary from lesson to lesson, class to class and school to school, the key elements will be common to all years and to all classroom contexts.
- Planning will be carried out on a weekly basis, with reference to the medium term planning grids in the Framework for Teaching Mathematics.
- In their direct teaching, with the whole class, in groups or with individuals and pairs, teachers will require simple practical resources. These will include large number lines, large number grids, medium number lines and small number grids, pupil sets of digit cards and place-value cards.

❷ The National Numeracy Strategy

The National Context

The National Numeracy Strategy follows the recommendations of the final report of the Numeracy Task Force (1998) that throughout the primary phase in education there should be:
- a daily mathematics lesson of 45 to 60 minutes
- a greatly increased proportion of whole class interactive direct teaching of mathematics
- a focus on teaching mental calculation strategies.

At the heart of the National Numeracy Strategy is the Framework for Teaching Mathematics. This document provides a structured sequence of teaching objectives for each year. Put simply, it outlines the mathematical content which must be taught to each school year group. Teachers are wholly aware of the necessity for teaching a structured sequence of skills to children, particularly in relation to developing effective mental calculation strategies (we are all familiar with the problem of teaching a topic, only to find that an essential pre-requisite skill has not been covered). The Framework provides just such a programme. Since September 1999, all schools in England have been expected either to draw upon the Framework for Teaching Mathematics in planning their lessons, or to ensure that their teaching programme covers a similarly complete and structured sequence of teaching objectives, with a focus on the development of mental calculation strategies.

2. The National Numeracy Strategy

The three-part lesson

In the National Numeracy Strategy and in Abacus, the daily mathematics lesson has the following three-part structure.

Part of lesson	What it comprises	Content includes	Abacus resources
Oral/ mental starter	• Usually number work • Sometimes related directly to the main teaching activity and sometimes not	• Counting (in steps of 1000, 50, 0·1, 0·5 etc.) • Strategies which have already been taught • Number facts (+, −, ×, ÷)	Mental Warm-up Activities Simmering Activities
Main teaching activity	One of the following: • Whole class introduction to the topic, using some paired work • Group work • Paired investigations • Individual practice	• Selected objectives from an appropriate year of the Framework for Teaching Mathematics	Teacher Cards Activity Book Textbooks Photocopy Masters
Plenary	• Validation and report on the work of children with whom you haven't worked directly • Rehearsal of main teaching objectives in the light of any common misconceptions • Explanation of the content to be covered next	• Summary of key objectives • Outline of objectives to be addressed next • Reinforcement activity • Possible homework activity	Teacher Cards Simmering Activities Homework Book

There is a variety of possible formats for the middle part of the lesson, depending on:
- where in the particular topic the lesson takes place (e.g. introducing a topic, continuing or extending a topic, assessing a topic, or revising a topic)
- the nature of the mathematical topic being taught
- the age and maturity of the children
- the nature of the classroom and school (e.g. mixed-age class, small rural school, large urban school, special school or unit).

The three-part structure is flexible, and is designed to accommodate teachers' individual teaching styles as well as differences in situation, organisation and content.

It is assumed (by the National Numeracy Strategy and by Abacus) that at the start of a topic there will be more whole class teaching, whereas in the middle or towards the end of a topic, there will be more directed teaching, focused on groups, pairs or individuals. However, over the topic as a whole, there will be a substantial proportion of direct teaching of the whole class (or of the whole year group in mixed-age classes).

3 Classroom management

The Teacher Card

For each unit of work the Teacher Card identifies for you:
- the direct teaching (introductory and follow-up) to the whole class or group
- whole class activities and small group differentiated activities
- appropriate Textbook pages, Photocopy Masters and Mental Warm-up Activities
- ideas for plenaries.

This enables you to plan effectively for the whole class (large or small), covering a wide range of ability.

Children will experience a range of tasks within each unit, the actual composition determined by you following the guidance on the Teacher Card.

Classroom organisation

Abacus allows for flexibility in the organisation of the children. On the assumption that the teaching takes place with the whole class, this can be followed using a variety of different organisational structures. Examples include:
- the whole class working together on the same activity, possibly in pairs
- half of the class working on one activity, whilst the other half work on another activity
- a 'carousel' of activities, with the children in groups, moving from one activity to another
- half of the children working in groups on activities, whilst the other half are working on material in the Textbooks or Photocopy Masters.

Organising groups

- You will decide on the best organisation of groups to suit your needs at any time. There should be no more than three levels of work in a single-age class, and no more than four levels in a mixed-age class.
- The composition of the groups will vary depending on the unit of work being studied.
- You can plan within your group structure, how, during the unit, you can work in a focused way with any one group.
- You will need to judge how much time to allow for different children to complete any task. The carousel nature of the tasks provides versatility in management.
- Other adults can be used to assist with the activities.
- Some children in the class may be used occasionally in a peer-tutoring role within the activity carousel.

4 The Abacus materials

Mental Warm-up Activities

The Mental Warm-up Activities Book provides a comprehensive scheme of work for developing mental mathematics strategies. Each day you will select an appropriate activity to take place before the main part of the lesson. The activities are designed to rehearse and sharpen key mental mathematics skills, including counting, comparing and ordering numbers. They allow you to get off to a clear, crisp start to the lesson.

Each unit includes a 'word of the week', 'shape of the week' or 'number of the week' which helps the children to extend their vocabulary and to begin to generate statements about familiar mathematical concepts.

N3 Multiplication/division

Table timer
Multiplying by 3, 6 and 12
A timer
Draw a table with four columns. In the left-hand column write the numbers 0 to 9 at random.
The children copy the table, multiplying by 3 and writing the answer in the first empty column, then multiplying by 6 and writing the answer in the next column, and finally multiplying by 12 and writing the answer in the right-hand column.
Time them. How quickly can they complete the table?

Number match
Multiplication facts
Number cards (0 to 9), cubes
Each pair writes a number from 2 to 9 on a piece of paper. Choose a child to take two cards at random and create a 2-digit number, e.g. 24. Each pair writes a multiplication fact that has this number as the answer, e.g. $3 \times 8 = 24$, $4 \times 6 = 24$, $2 \times 12 = 24$. Write all the multiplication facts on the board. Any pair whose original number appears in one of the multiplication facts may claim a cube. Repeat, choosing another child to take two number cards. Continue until one pair has collected ten cubes.

Number of the week 2587

Sample tasks	• Round this number to its nearest hundred. How far away is it?
	• Round this number to its nearest ten. How far away is it?
	• Is it nearer to 2550 or 2600, 2000 or 3000, ...?
Sample facts	• It is between 2000 and 3000.
	• It cannot be divided by 5, or 10, or 3, or 2, ...
	• It has two odd digits and two even digits.

Teacher Cards

The main teaching for the lesson is supported by the Teacher Cards. The front of each Teacher Card provides:
- support for the whole class teaching on the first day of a topic
- a list of the key teaching points addressed by the Unit
- a list of any materials necessary for the teaching
- key vocabulary either introduced or used during the course of the Unit.

N3 Multiplication/division

Teaching points
- To mentally recall multiplication facts up to 10×10
- To multiply by zero
- To mentally derive corresponding division facts

Materials
- Strips of paper 66 cm by 6 cm, each divided equally into a strip of eleven 6 cm by 6 cm squares (one per pair)
- Blu-tack

Key words
- multiple
- times
- multiply
- divide

Teaching
- Rehearse the multiples of 5 by chanting them together, starting with zero. *Zero, five, ten, fifteen, ...* Repeat for the multiples of different numbers.
- Give out the strips, one per pair. Give each pair a set of multiples from the 1s to the 10s. The children write the multiples, one per square along the strip, using large numerals. They start with '0'. For example, a pair who are writing the multiples of 3 write '0, 3, 6, 9 ... 30' along their strip.
- When all the strips are completed, ask a pair with the multiples of 1 to bring out their strip. Blu-tack it as the top row on the board. Next, choose a pair with the multiples of 2 to stick their strip directly below the first, to create the second row. Continue until the ten rows have been arranged to create a multiplication square.
- Write '$4 \times 6 =$' on the board. Read it together. *Four times six ...? Four sixes ...?* Point to the row showing multiples of 6. *Zero sixes, one six, two sixes, three sixes, four sixes.* Point as you go to reach 24. *Four sixes are twenty-four.* Write '24'.
- Repeat this for different multiplication facts, encouraging the children to try to recall the answer, before referring to the multiples as a check.
- Write '$0 \times 7 =$' on the board. Read it together. *Zero times seven ...? No sevens ...?* Point to the multiples of 7 to demonstrate. Write '0'. *No sevens are zero.*
- Write '$35 \div 7 =$' on the board. Read it together. *Thirty-five divided by seven is ...? How many sevens make thirty-five ...?* Point to the row showing multiples of 7. *Zero sevens, one seven, ... five sevens.* Point as you go to reach 35. *Five sevens are thirty-five.* Write '35'.
- Repeat for different division facts, again encouraging the children to try to recall the answer before using the grid on the board to help.

4. The Abacus materials

The back of each Teacher Card provides:
- support for further teaching for a subsequent day
- references to differentiated practical activities, including materials and learning outcomes (which are presented in a separate Activity Book)
- guidance on key points, common misconceptions, and so on, for use during plenary sessions
- references to additional Abacus resources: Mental Warm-up Activities, Activity Book, Textbooks, Photocopy Masters.

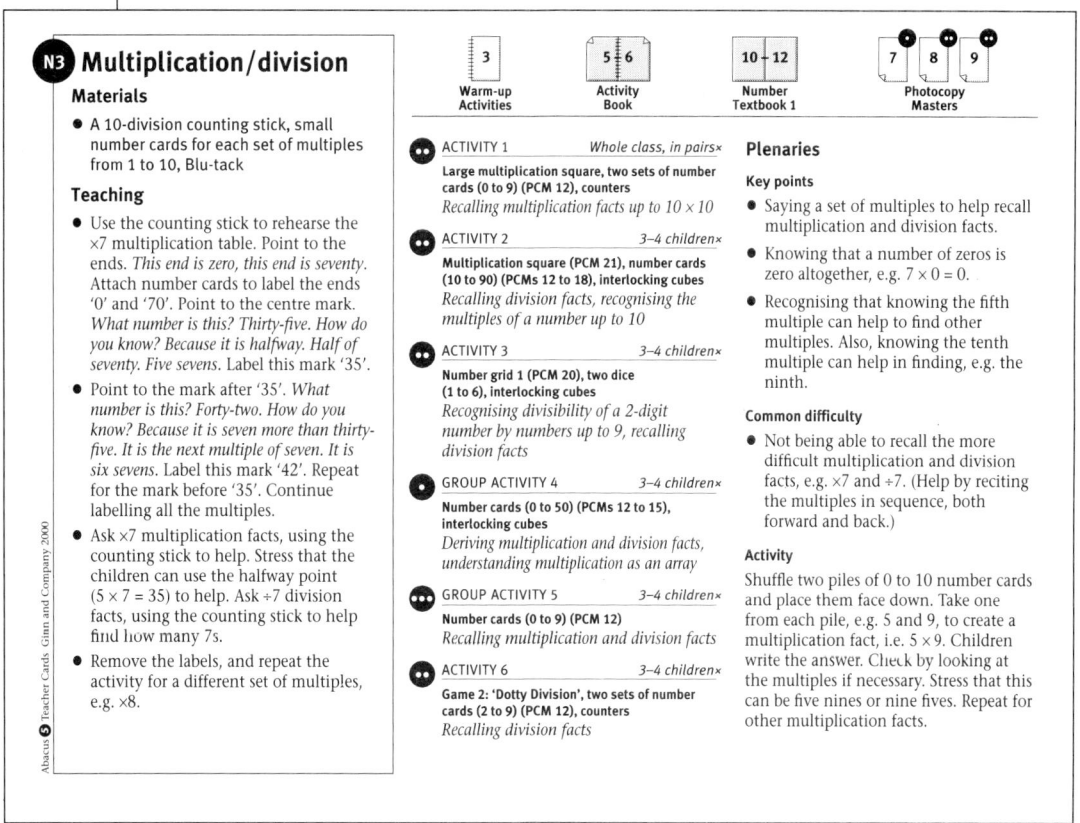

The Teacher Cards are divided into two sets: *Number* and *Shape, Data and Measures*. A suggested teaching order, and how this fits with the National Numeracy Framework Planning Grids are given at the end of this book. There are other possible routes through the materials, and the *Shape, Data and Measures* units are presented in a separate block to allow you to re-order them easily.

4. The Abacus materials

Activity Book

The Activity Book includes all the practical activities which will follow the introductory teaching. Each Unit of the programme is supported by a range of activities, covering different styles, learning objectives, numbers of children and resources, which are fully referenced on each Teacher Card. Most Units include an activity which may be taught to the whole class. Such activities are indicated by the icon:

For each Unit, there are also two group activities presented in a photocopiable format that can be presented directly to the pupils. These encourage language development by allowing pupils to interpret instructions themselves.

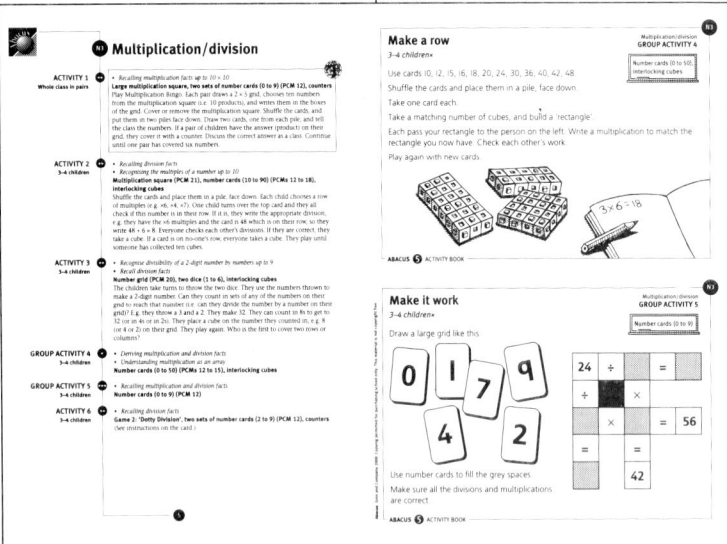

Each activity includes the following information:
- appropriate number of children
- a list of relevant materials and 'specialist' resources (provided as Photocopy Masters at the back of the book)
- level of difficulty, indicated by a simple code:
  - ● basic work
  - ●● for all children
  - ●●● enrichment and extension
- learning points are also provided – these will assist the teacher in directing the group and in making informal assessments.

A number of ICT activities are included (these assume some prior knowledge of relevant software, e.g. spreadsheets).

Textbooks

There are three Textbooks in Abacus 5, two for *Number* and one for *Shape, Data and Measures*. Each Textbook page offers consolidation of the practical work covered by you and gives evidence of the children's progress through the scheme.

The instructions on the pages are contained in speech bubbles. This has the dual function of keeping text to a minimum, as well as aiding readability. Key mathematical vocabulary is

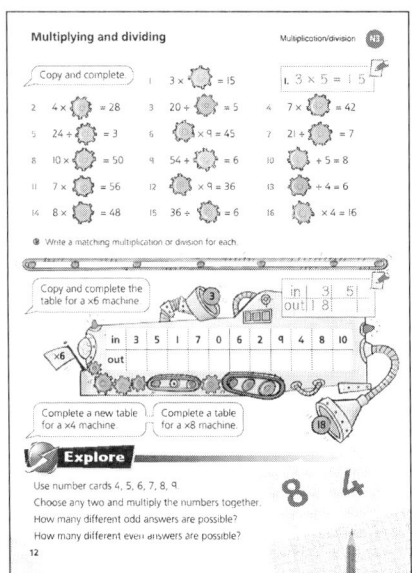

reinforced throughout. A key feature of the pages is the inclusion of 'Extras' (coded ☻) and 'Explores', which provide additional activities usually with an investigational or practical focus away from the Textbook page. Word problems are also included throughout the Textbooks in 'Problems' sections. Relevant Textbook pages are referenced on each Teacher Card.

4. The Abacus materials

Photocopy Masters

The Photocopy Masters contain activities to enhance the children's learning and are referenced on the relevant Teacher Cards. They include:
- more work for reinforcement
- extension and enrichment material
- games, and other shared, practical activities.

The Photocopy Masters are coded in the same way as the practical activities: ● basic work, ● for all children, ●● enrichment and extension.

Resource Bank and Games Pack

The Resource Bank provides the essential materials needed for the teaching and practical activities in the programme. The basic resources you need for Year 5 are recommended on page 34, but the Resource Bank gives you the flexibility to order additional sets of materials to suit your particular needs. Items include: group and class sets of number cards, place-value cards, wall charts and number line cards.

The Games Pack provides eight games aimed at practising skills relating to specific Teacher Card units. They are referenced as activities in the Activity Book.

Simmering Activities

Relevant quick-recalls, games and other activities are contained in the Upper Junior Simmering Activities book. The activities require little or no preparation and are brief enough to be carried out in just a few minutes – at registration or in the dinner queue. Once introduced, the activity can be used regularly to allow the concept or skill to keep 'simmering'.

4. The Abacus materials

Homework Book

The Homework Book provides a valuable opportunity for shared activities between the parent and child. A range of activities are included
(shared mathematics tasks, games, memorisation activities, investigative or problem-solving activities), one for each Unit of the programme. Some activities are more formal practice, whilst others are more informal shared activities.

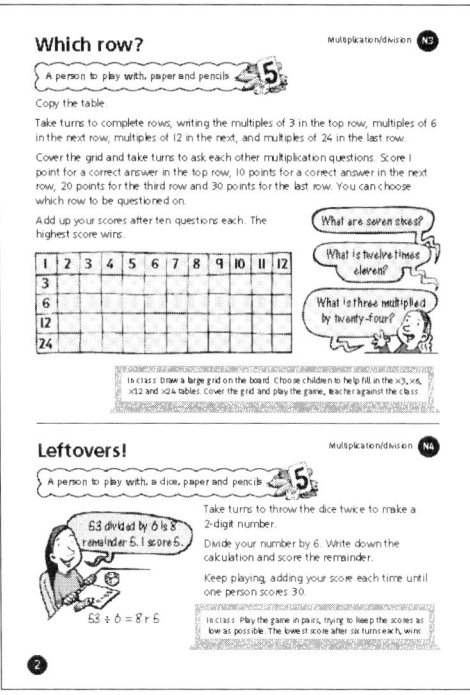

Assessment Book

The Assessment Book provides photocopiable assessment sheets, and teacher guidance for each Unit of the programme. The teacher's notes include a summary of the skills assessed, diagnostic advice, activities for children who require further consolidation and oral mental maths questions.

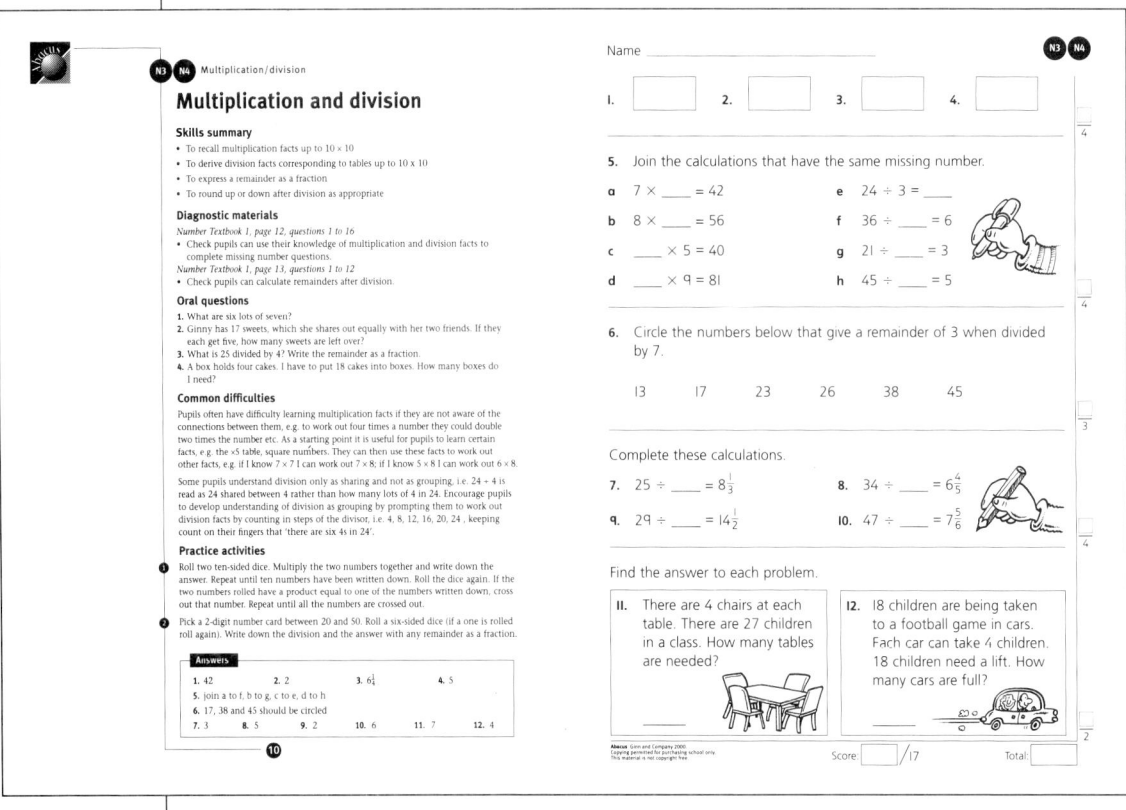

4. The Abacus materials

Challenge Book

The Challenge Book is aimed at pupils requiring further enrichment and extension within a Unit. The Challenge Book provides a photocopiable sheet, and teacher's notes for each Unit, so that more able children will either:
- extend their mathematical understanding beyond the focus of the Unit
- broaden their understanding of the particular topic they are studying.

The challenges require minimal teacher input and use very few additional materials.

Numeracy Support Book

The Numeracy Support Book is aimed specifically at those pupils who are having difficulty with their number work. The book outlines appropriate skills, teaching strategies, activities and follow-up work. It is divided into sections dealing with key mathematical skills.

Each section provides a step-by-step progression of teaching strategies, a range of tactics and a bank of straightforward practical activities. Follow-up work in the form of photocopy masters provides carefully graded practice of the specific numerical skills.

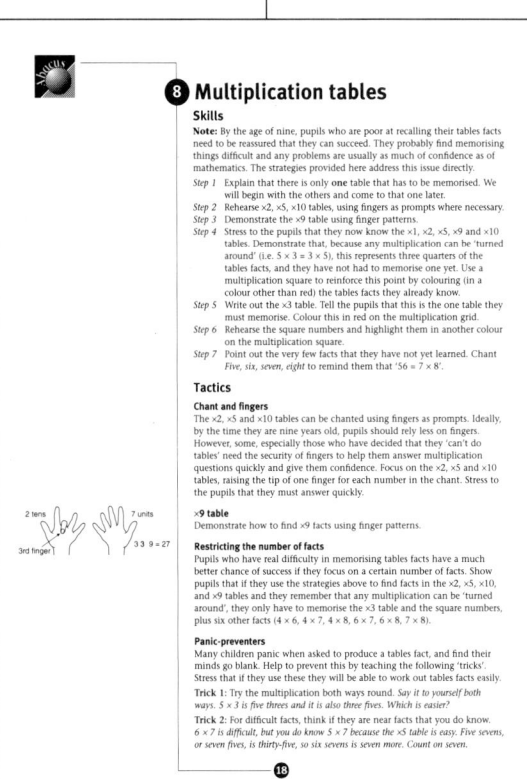

5 An Abacus Unit

Abacus was conceived with the identical approach to teaching as the National Numeracy Strategy. The New Abacus Unit matches precisely the structure of a sequence of linked three-part lessons through a topic. As an illustration, the planning for a typical Year 5 lesson is shown below.

	Day 1	Day 2	Day 3
Mental/oral starter	Practise a necessary pre-requisite skill, e.g. multiples of 5 that add to 100.	Rehearse number pairs (or bonds) to 100 to help with quick arithmetic.	Play a 'bingo' game, adding to 3-digit numbers to make the next multiple of 100.
Main teaching activity	1. Introduce topic to whole class, using a 100-division number line as a model and demonstrate how to find pairs to 100 for any 2-digit number e.g. 43 + 57 = 100, then what must be added to a 3-digit number to make the next multiple of 100, e.g. 643 + 57 = 700. 2. Children all do brief practice activity, teacher working with least able group.	1. Briefly rehearse the main teaching point, using the number line. 2. Children work in four groups. Teacher works with less able children, providing a hands-on activity and further teaching. 'Middle' two groups work independently on written practice. More able children work on an extension activity.	1. Rehearse the main teaching point, using a different model (e.g. 10p and 1p coins, place-value cards). 2. Children work in pairs and individually on a graded task using money and/or place-value cards as appropriate, and recording their work in their mathematics book. 3. Assess children's work, looking at how far they progressed with graded tasks.
Plenary	Rehearse the main point and play a game to practise the method.	Feedback from middle two groups and more able to whole class. Address some common difficulties.	Rehearse main teaching point through common difficulty. Summarise what the children have learned.

5. An Abacus Unit

Immediately it is clear that the Abacus materials have been designed to fit the structure shown in the above topic plan.

	Day 1	Day 2	Day 3
Mental/oral starter	Mental Warm-up Activities *(Practise a necessary pre-requisite skill)*	Mental Warm-up Activities *(Rehearse number pairs)*	Mental Warm-up Activities *(Play a 'bingo' game)*
Main teaching activity	1. Teacher Card front *(Introduce topic to whole class)* 2. Activity Book and number grids *(Brief practice activity)*	1. Teacher Card front and first activity (whole class) *(Rehearse the main teaching point)* 2. Activities from the Activity Book, Textbooks, Photocopy Masters *(Children work in four groups)*	1. Teacher Card back *(Rehearse the main teaching point, using different model)* 2. Textbook and/or Activity Book *(Children work in pairs and individually on a graded task)* 3. Assessment book *(Assess children's work)*
Plenary	Teacher Card back *(Rehearse the main point and play a game)*	Teacher Card back *(Address some common difficulties)*	Teacher Card back *(Rehearse main teaching point through common difficulty)*

Supporting teachers in teaching and children in learning

Abacus is founded on the idea that teachers need to be in control of how and when they teach a particular piece of mathematics to their class. It is the teacher, and not the materials, who makes the professional decisions. Therefore the Abacus materials have been designed to allow you to decide:
- how long to spend on any one topic
- how to structure that topic – the proportion of time spent on whole class teaching, group work, individual or paired practice, assessment and revision
- how to time the different parts of the lesson – the length of mental/oral sections, direct teaching, practice
- the order in which to teach the topics
- how to relate the teaching of number and non-number topics.

5. An Abacus Unit

Flexibility in the teaching of each topic

Whilst the Abacus planning grids (from page 42) have been designed to match the medium term planning grids in the Numeracy Framework, a degree of flexibility is nevertheless built in. Abacus allows you to structure each topic as you see fit. Some topics may be completed in two days, and some will run over three days, and it is up to you how long to remain on any one topic. In Abacus, as in the Framework, there is often a sequence of related topics, and the practice of some of the key skills may therefore continue over two, or even three, topics. This allows for the maximum reinforcement of the basic skills and facts.

Flexibility in classroom management

The basic Abacus model enables you to decide how best to structure the main teaching activity. Each Teacher Card is structured to provide a minimum of two whole class teaching sessions, drawing upon different models or images in demonstrating the topic to the children. The Activity Book supplies a variety of activities, from those for use with the whole class to those directed at small groups or pairs. The Textbooks and Photocopy Masters allow for structured and appropriate levels of practice, and again these can be used individually or in pairs, or to structure some group work. The activities in the Assessment Book enable teachers to structure their own assessment and evaluation tasks, and to practise the skills needed for the Standard Tasks and Tests at the end of each Key Stage.

Teaching in mixed-age classes

The order of the Abacus Teacher Cards matches closely the order of topics outlined in the medium term planning grids in the Numeracy Framework. This means that there is a planned overlap in the order of topics for years 1, 2 and 3, and also for years 4, 5 and 6. It is therefore quite possible to plan and teach a topic to two or more year groups, moving across from one set of objectives to another.

With Abacus, the organisation of this becomes quite simple. You select the appropriate Teacher Cards from each year, e.g. Years 5 and 6. The pre-requisite skills for these cards will then allow you to select a mental/oral activity which can be carried out with the whole class (from the Mental Warm-up Activities for Years 5 or 6). You can then move on to some direct teaching, following the selected Year 5 Teacher Card. (The Year 6 children can either participate as a recap, or work independently on a prepared activity.) Later, or on the second day, it will be possible to move on to some direct teaching with Year 6, from the appropriate Teacher Card, whilst Year 5 children are engaged in relevant follow-up work.

5. An Abacus Unit

Starting the lesson

As we know, the way a lesson starts can often dictate the direction of subsequent teaching. If a lesson gets off to a crisp, clear start, the children are likely to be well prepared to engage with the main topic being taught. The National Numeracy Strategy suggests that the first ten minutes of the lesson should be allocated to the practice and reinforcement of those skills and facts which benefit from a 'little and often' approach. In this category are included:

- counting in steps of different sizes, both forwards and backwards
- instant recall of number facts, including discussing ways of remembering the facts that need to be learned by heart
- previously-taught mental strategies.

It is not appropriate to introduce topics for the first time in this mental/oral part of the lesson, and neither should complex operations be explained. It is a time for 'quick-fire' rehearsal of basic skills, for using a strategy that has already been taught, or for choosing an operation to solve a problem quickly.

This part of the session will almost always be number work, although occasionally it may focus on a particular aspect of shape or of measures, such as 'time'. Importantly, it is not necessarily related to the second part of the lesson. For example, a teacher planning a lesson on 2-d shape could (and often would) include a starter activity on number.

This part of the lesson involves working with the whole class and only exceptionally would it be necessary to work with a group or to exempt individuals from the session. The Abacus Mental Warm-up Activities have been specifically written to address this part of the lesson, and provide a wide variety of whole class oral and mental activities for each day's teaching.

Main teaching activity

The function of the main part of the lesson can vary, depending upon various factors (where you are in a topic, the age and maturity of the children etc.). It can provide time for:

- introducing a new topic
- extending previous work and developing children's understanding
- practising a skill or strategy
- using and applying what has been learned
- assessing children's learning
- revising or revisiting a topic.

During the main teaching activity, the teacher can choose how to organise the class. It is quite possible that the lesson you teach on a

5. An Abacus Unit

Monday will have quite a different style of classroom organisation from the lesson you teach on Tuesday. Clearly, the way you choose to organise the class will be guided by the purpose of the lesson (is it introducing a new topic, or rehearsing an old one?). It will also dictate, to some extent, the teaching strategy you use. For example, a whole class lesson could require a higher percentage of demonstration or explanation, whilst a lesson where groups of children are working together could involve more discussion or description. Taking all these factors into account, on any one day a teacher can choose to organise the class:

- as a whole class session, with direct teaching of the whole class or with a paired investigation
- with the children working in groups, and the teacher working in a focused way with one or two of the groups
- with the children working on a task in pairs or as individuals.

Although the Numeracy Strategy explicitly encourages a flexible approach to the organisation of the main teaching activity, it is clear about three central points:

- the need for teachers to organise the class to fit the purpose of the lesson
- that, although any one lesson may not involve a high proportion of direct teaching of the whole class (or year group) nevertheless, over the complete unit, more than 50% of the teaching is likely to be of this form
- that emphasis should be placed on keeping the children together, so it would not be appropriate to set more than three levels of work for any one year group, and no more than two levels of work per year group in a mixed-age range class (though, clearly, specific provision must be made for particular children who have individual education plans).

It is clear (from the National Numeracy Strategy) that at the heart of the teaching and learning process is the active, direct teaching of a topic. In order to focus on this, teachers need to have:

- a clear objective for each lesson and a set of objectives for the topic
- a definite 'way of teaching' – an image or model (e.g. number line, money) which will be used to represent or demonstrate the mathematics
- a variety of teaching strategies to ensure that the lesson is interactive.

The Abacus Teacher Cards have been designed with these three requirements in mind.

- They provide a clear set of objectives for each unit, with specific learning objectives for each activity.
- They outline the model to be used in teaching the mathematics, and make clear the careful use of vocabulary.
- They also provide a variety of teaching strategies, through the work with the whole class, the group activities, the individual and paired practice and the extra support provided by the Simmering Activities and the Games.

5. An Abacus Unit

The plenary session

Plenary sessions can often be the hardest part of the lesson to teach successfully. The children (and the teacher!) are tired, and some will require more feedback than others, meaning that boredom may cause disruption. It is hard to plan the plenary session because it will often develop from what has occurred during the lesson.

The purpose of the plenary as explained by the Numeracy Strategy is threefold. It allows time for the following elements.
- A rehearsal of the main teaching points and summary of the key facts. This is the vital, 'What have we learned today?' part of the lesson.
- Children to present their work to you and others, particularly those who may have been working independently during the main part of the lesson.
- Addressing any difficulties that may have arisen during the lesson.
- Forward planning – helping to make explicit what we are going to do next, and perhaps outlining any homework.

Rehearsing the main teaching points of the lesson is very important for two reasons. Firstly, it allows you to ensure that the learning objectives have been clearly articulated and that children have taken this in. Secondly, it enables you to pick up any difficulties that several children may have shared. Frequently there will be common misconceptions or errors which it can prove useful to address with the whole class. This is not to point out children who have made mistakes, but rather to use common errors as a way of rehearsing the teaching points.

The Abacus Teacher Cards highlight the key learning points and also provide advice on probable common misconceptions which may occur when teaching that particular topic. This will allow you to plan how to address such misconceptions, as well as preparing you to look out for difficulties which are encountered by several children.

Taking feedback from children is difficult to do in a way which does not leave some of the class feeling bored or frustrated. It helps to vary the format of their presentation. For example:
- ask some children to write a question they had to do on the board
- give some children a poster or a strip of paper to record some or all of their work during an activity, so that they can display this
- ask a group to show their work and then choose a question to ask the rest of the class
- choose a pair of children to demonstrate a strategy they have been using
- choose some children to write the answer to a question on the board. The rest of the class have to guess what the question was.

The plenary can also be made easier by discussing a group of children's work with them, and then marking it together just before you bring the whole class together. That group can then show the class their work by showing any pieces you felt were particularly special.

5. An Abacus Unit

The plenary should end with a suggestion about where the children are going next in mathematics. You may be going to extend the work you did today, or start a new topic. Sometimes you will want to give the class a formal homework task, and on other occasions it will be a more informal activity (e.g. *Look out for car numbers with digits that total 15. Can you remember one to tell me tomorrow?*).

The plenary should be kept short – a protracted ending will not improve the lesson or make the children learn any more. The lesson needs to be brought to a sharp close, and the plenary enables the teacher to evaluate its success.

Homework

It is important to bear in mind the purposes of homework. A reasonable list might include:
- To involve the parents in their children's learning.
- To help parents keep abreast of what their child can and cannot do.
- To utilise the context of the home and apply some numerical strategies in a non-school situation.
- To encourage parents and children to talk about their number work and for children to explain what they are doing and how.
- To extend the time for learning mathematics and give some extra practice in number work.
- To help parents improve, extend or practise their own numerical strategies.

It is a well-established fact that simply sending home extra mathematics will have little or no effect on many children's attainment, unless effort is made to involve and include their parents in their learning. Therefore, in planning and setting homework, it is important that schools consider the following points.

How much and how often?

Little and fairly frequently is better than lots occasionally. It is good to have specific and regular homework 'nights' so that parents and children grow to expect it. An ideal schedule is a shared task at the weekend, so that parents can get involved, and more traditional individual homework once or twice a week, depending on the age of the child.

What type?

Homework is most effective when it is varied – some types of homework might include:
- Shared mathematics tasks, games or other activities where the child discusses the mathematics. The task itself might draw upon the home context.
- Memorisation games or activities to help children with the instant recall of number facts.
- Tasks or activities which help children practise number strategies or skills introduced in school.
- Investigative or problem-solving activities where the child, and the parent, explore an aspect of mathematics together.

5. An Abacus Unit

The Abacus Homework Books have been planned to include a range of these types of activity. How many parents get involved with the shared activities is not only dependent on the catchment area of the school – research indicates that the attitude of the teachers and the school is a very important factor. By holding meetings, talking to parents, feeding back information and trying to keep them involved, the school can make a huge difference to the number of parents who play an active role in their child's education.

Who is it for?

All children can be encouraged to share mathematics activities with their parents (though the proportion of homework to be done independently will increase as children get older). However, no child should be excluded from an activity because they have difficulty finding a partner to share the task at home. Wherever possible provision for repeating or extending the shared task in the context of school (or at an after school club) should be made.

Assessment

Opportunities for informal assessment occur throughout many of the aspects of an Abacus Unit.

The Mental Warm-up Activities offer opportunities for observational assessment, both for the whole class and for individuals. The continuous feedback in the form of child response to these tasks provides immediate observational measures of performance. The opportunities in this stage of the unit for you to set tasks for varying levels of ability inform further when assessing the feedback. Similarly, during the Plenary sessions, observational assessment opportunities are numerous.

Additional opportunities are provided during the main teaching, both during the interactive element of the teaching, and particularly when the children are engaged in group activities, and you are focusing on a chosen group.

Assessment of the children's written work is provided from completed Textbook pages and Photocopy Masters and can be recorded using the Assessment grids on pages 36 to 39.

The Assessment Book offers comprehensive support material for assessing children's progress, within each unit or small set of units. This range includes: a written assessment sheet, oral assessment questions, and suggested sections of the Textbook to use for diagnostic purposes. Also included are common difficulties, and suggested practical activities to help overcome these.

6 Differentiation

The National Numeracy Strategy emphasises the need to keep the children together. This links to the requirement that, over a period of time, the proportion of whole class direct teaching should be more than 50% (indeed, it is easy to see how this figure could be closer to 75% in a single year group, given that the mental starter and plenary both involve working with the whole class).

Whole class focus

Although any one lesson may not involve a high proportion of whole class direct teaching, over a complete topic, more than 50% of the teaching is likely to be with the whole class.

Keeping the children together

Emphasis should be placed on keeping the children together, so that it would not be appropriate to set more than three levels of work for any one year group, and no more than two levels of work per year group in a mixed-age class. Clearly, specific provision must be made for particular children who have individual education plans.

This marks a change in attitude to teaching the class, and has repercussions for record-keeping and assessment plans. Given that we are now:
- teaching the same topic to all the children
- practising pre-requisite skills in the mental/oral starter with all the children
- dividing into no more than three groups for the main part of the lesson

it is no longer necessary to write notes on the progress of every single child. The majority of each year group will be engaged in the same tasks, and studying the same mathematics at the same level. For these children, it is important to record deviations from the norm: i.e. what happens if the child was not able to cope with the work given, or if they found it too easy.

It remains as true as ever that children are individuals, who do not all learn or develop at the same rate. The following points may help teachers to cope with the inevitable differences between children when they are teaching the whole class and 'keeping all the children together'.

It is important to remember that the class may be divided into more than three *groups* as long as there are no more than three *levels* of work. Most teachers organise their class so that the children are seated in small groups. They may, therefore, have two or three 'tables' working at the same level, probably on the same activity. One or two more or less able children may be working on an activity more appropriate for their ability.

6. Differentiation

Once the topic has been introduced to the children, and the main direct teaching has taken place, it is usual to split the class into groups for most of them to work more independently, and to practise or apply what they have just been taught. It is only in this way that children come to make this knowledge their own. It is also the means of finding out who has, and who has not, grasped the mathematics, and therefore assessing the need for further teaching or practice. It is a sensible strategy to work with the children who need most help first, since this is the group who are likely to need some further teaching before they are able to work independently or semi-independently on the topic.

There is (as the Numeracy Strategy makes clear) a 'hierarchy' of types of work which can be used when planning for groups of children. It is easiest for children to do work which has been laid out for them, and where few decisions have to be made about what is to be done. Thus Textbooks, where the children are given help with laying out their work, and the tasks are still well-defined, are also useful in enabling independent work. Photocopy Masters are also relatively simple for children to use independently from the teacher. Work written on the board is more difficult, since children must lay it out for themselves. Activities involving structural materials, coins, number cards, grids, etc., can require quite a high input from the teacher.

Abacus provides materials for the different levels of work suggested by the Numeracy Strategy and also helps to organise the class so that you are working in a focused way with one group, as recommended. The Activity Book indicates activities targeted at three ability levels, and the Textbooks allow for children who find the work moderately easy to engage with extension activities. It is easiest to organise the class so that those children who are working relatively independently have suitably contained activities – (e.g. Photocopy Masters, Textbooks), whilst those children who have the benefit of your focused attention engage in the activities which enable further directed teaching.

Special needs

Children who have Individual Education Plans (IEPs) will normally be included in the whole class parts of the lesson, such as the mental/oral starter, the plenary, and the introduction to the topic in the main teaching activity. It will be rare for a child to be excluded from these parts of the lesson, although behaviour management, or their skills level, may mean that they are only present for some of these activities. Once a topic has been introduced, the teacher will need to ensure that the follow-up activities are at a level which is appropriate for the child and which fit with their development plan. Normally children with IEPs will work on the same topic as the remainder of the class, but at a lower level or by addressing some of the pre-requisite skills needed to engage with that topic. This work can be selected either from the Abacus Unit itself, drawing upon appropriate activities, or from appropriate sections of the Numeracy Support Book.

7 Teaching strategies

Abacus is conceived around the conviction that active teaching is at the heart of an effective mathematics lesson. Although most teachers never analyse what they do, teaching in fact includes a number of different components. Good, lively and direct teaching involves:
- Demonstrating or modelling a strategy or skill. This can include showing children how to do something or providing an image to help them to understand a strategy.
- Instructing, or talking children through a procedure or process to be followed.
- Explaining and illustrating – providing reasons and giving examples.
- Questioning and discussing, so that teachers actively encourage children's engagement with mathematics.
- Practising, rehearsing and reinforcing a skill or a set of operations. Teachers use repetition to increase familiarity, and practice to help consolidation of strategies or procedures.
- Evaluating children's responses and dealing with errors.

In order to teach a good lesson, you need to have a clear sense of **what** you are teaching and **how** to teach it, using a set of strategies. This means knowing which images or resources can be used to demonstrate or model a particular mathematical concept or operation. The Abacus Teacher Cards outline the objectives clearly, so that you know precisely what is being covered in each Unit. It can be a good idea to share a key objective with the children, often writing it at the top of the flipchart or board. *Today, we are going to learn how to add ten or twenty or thirty to a number.*

The Teacher Card also describes the images or models which can be used to teach each topic effectively (the Abacus authors have brought a great deal of expertise and effort to bear in this area). Teachers can be confident of having a range of ways to represent or demonstrate the mathematics involved, to enable children to understand and apply what they are learning.

When teaching young children, it is almost always possible to break down the representation of a piece of mathematics into two stages. First, children need a model – a way of understanding the appropriate mathematical concept. Second, they need to be shown how to perform the operation involved.

For example, when beginning to teach addition we want children to understand that addition is not only about combining two sets of objects, but also about counting on along a number line. So, 5 + 2 can be modelled by adding two bricks to a tower of five (making it more likely that children will count on from '5', rather than counting the bricks in the first tower). Addition will also be modelled using a number line or track,

7. Teaching strategies

starting from 5 and counting on two more. The towers and the number line both provide a representation of the mathematics involved. They enable children to make sense of what they are being taught and to hold visual images in their heads.

However, children also need a practical and easy way of doing any appropriate additions. In this example, they will almost certainly be taught how to use fingers to count on when performing additions (relating back to the model, e.g. the number line). *Start at 5 and count on two more, using fingers. Six, seven. The answer is seven.* The demonstration or modelling uses the towers of bricks or the number line, but the method of doing the additions will use fingers.

Abacus draws upon a wide variety of models, images and strategies to demonstrate and explain the mathematical concepts and operations which children encounter. These include:
- number lines 1 to 100, and beyond
- number grids (0 to 99 or 1 to 100)
- small digit cards
- interlocking cubes in sets of ten, and loose cubes
- place-value cards
- money, particularly £1, 10p and 1p coins to help with place-value.

In addition, Abacus develops a number of effective and pragmatic strategies for children to use when performing mathematical operations, such as adding two numbers. These include:
- fingers – used to help count, count on or back, double numbers, learn number pairs for numbers up to and including ten, count in twos, fives and tens, and recognise odd and even numbers
- number lines or tracks – used to help count on, find a difference, count back, compare numbers, round to the nearest multiple of ten
- number grids (0 to 99 or 1 to 100) – used to help count to 100, add or subtract tens or multiples of ten, count in steps of various sizes, compare numbers or to find the next multiple of ten
- place-value cards – used to help compare numbers and understand the value of each digit.

Questioning

There are two types of question which are used in teaching mathematics – open questions and closed questions. Open questions are generally addressed to the whole class. Closed questions can be targeted at particular children (though they too can be addressed to a large group). You need to consider which type of question is most likely to achieve the response you require, as well as which will serve the mathematical end you have in mind. It is often true that a question asked in an 'open' form will achieve a much higher degree of interaction than the same question if asked in a closed format. For example, a closed question might be *What*

7. Teaching strategies

adds to 3 to make 10? whereas a more open question would be *Who can tell me two numbers which add together to make 10?* The first question has only one answer, but the second can be used to generate a response from every pair of children in the room.

How do you expect the children to respond to your questions?
The traditional mode of teacher question and pupil answer, where children wave their hands in the air and one child is selected to answer, can result in frustrated children and only a few of the class taking part. Recent trials show that teachers are increasingly drawing on a range of resources in encouraging all the children in the class to respond to a question. The children can:

- use number cards, holding these up to show an answer
- all suggest answers, so that the teacher then records lots of different answers on the flipchart or board and then rehearses the operation with the class to see which answer is correct
- keep an answer hidden and then reveal it on a count of three
- all say or shout an answer in unison – particularly where an answer which you hope is on 'automatic pilot' is required, such as *Four and what make ten?*
- work in pairs to write down an answer, and then hand in papers (without names on).

We know, from the evidence of both research and practice over recent years, that questions and answers can provide a valuable means of creating an interactive teaching environment. One useful strategy is to give each child a 'maths partner' to work with in short bursts in question and answer sessions, or when playing whole class games. The first time the class work with their pairs may prove difficult, but they will soon start working well together and you will notice great improvements in their speaking and listening.

8 Specific guidance on mathematical content

Introducing Abacus

Abacus may be introduced to a whole school at once, or it may be started with a class of pupils who have come from other schools, and who have not previously been working with the Abacus approach.

In order to help those teachers who are introducing Abacus to children for the first time, these key skills are an assumed foundation for the children entering Year 5.

- To count on or back in tens or hundreds from any 3- or 4-digit number
- To read, write and order 4-digit numbers
- To know what each digit represents in a 4-digit number
- To know addition and subtraction facts for each number up to 20
- To recall addition pairs to 10, 20, and 100, e.g. 4 + 6 = 10, 13 + 7 = 20, 45 + 55 = 100
- To mentally add three or more 1-digit numbers
- To mentally add a multiple of 10 or 100, or near multiple of 10 or 100 to a 3-digit number
- To mentally subtract a multiple of 10 or 100, or near multiple of 10 or 100 from a 3-digit number
- To recognise and find unit ($\frac{1}{2}$, $\frac{1}{3}$, ...) and non-unit ($\frac{2}{3}$, $\frac{4}{3}$, ...) fractions of shapes and amounts
- To recognise decimal notation and place-value for tenths and hundredths
- To recall ×2, ×3, ×4, ×5 and ×10 multiplication facts
- To recognise division as the inverse of multiplication
- To recall doubles of numbers up to 50, and corresponding halves
- To understand and use £·p notation, e.g. £4·25
- To know the relationship between units of time: second, minute, hour, day, week, month, year
- To read times on analogue and digital clocks to the nearest minute
- To know the relationship between units of length, weight and capacity
- To identify right angles
- To recognise the relationship between right angles and degree measure
- To measure and calculate perimeter and area using standard units
- To identify lines of symmetry in simple shapes
- To recognise and name common 2-d shapes (square, rectangle, circle, triangle, pentagon, hexagon,...)
- To recognise and name common 3-d shapes (cube, cuboid, pyramid, cone, sphere, cylinder,...)
- To recognise and use the eight-point compass directions

In order to get the best out of the Abacus materials, you are advised to note the following points.

8. Specific guidance on mathematical content

Place-value

At Key Stage 1, children need to develop a solid foundation in the understanding of the place-value aspect of our number system, progressing from tens and units to hundreds, tens and units. They need to understand that the '4' in 47, for example, stands for four tens, that 47 lies between the 'tens' forty and fifty, and that it is nearer to fifty. 'Place-value' cards are suggested as a model to aid this understanding, alongside Base 10 material. In Year 2 children will begin to become familiar with 3-digit numbers.

In Year 3 children will consolidate their familiarity with 3-digit numbers, and in Year 4 they extend this to 4-digit numbers. They will locate the position of numbers on number lines, leading to the concept of rounding numbers to their nearest ten and nearest hundred.

In Year 5 children are encouraged to extend their knowledge of place-value, both to numbers with more than four digits, and to decimal numbers with one or two decimal places. Tenths and hundredths are modelled using 10-division and 100-division number lines. Place-value cards are extended to include both tenths cards and hundredths cards, used with the whole number cards.

Addition and subtraction

Abacus places strong emphasis on the development of children's mental addition and subtraction skills, and children are taught a variety of strategies to enhance this development. The emphasis placed on reciting numbers in sequence lays the foundation for using the strategies of counting on and counting back to add and subtract. The number line and the 1 to 100 number grid are frequently used to model both addition and subtraction.

Many mental addition and subtraction skills depend on a sound knowledge of addition pairs (or bonds) to 10, to 20, to 100, for example. Abacus places a great emphasis on the recognition of addition pairs to 10 and 20 in Key Stage 1. This means more than knowing that, for example, 13 and 7 make 20, but includes the child being able to respond immediately with one member of the 'pair', when hearing the other.

Abacus encourages a carefully structured development in the use of appropriate vocabulary associated with addition and subtraction. The long term aim is for children to recognise all the different ways of reading the '+' and '−' signs, and the '=' sign. The vocabulary suggested on the Teacher Cards develops with this aim in view.

The grounding established at Key Stage 1 provides the platform for extension towards knowing addition pairs to 100 in Years 3 and 4, particularly when the two numbers are multiples of 10, e.g. 30 and 70, or multiples of 5, e.g. 35 and 65. This progresses to any 2-digit numbers, e.g. 27 and 63. These skills are rehearsed in Year 5, then extended to include addition pairs to 1 and 10, when the pairs are 1-place decimals. Links between subtraction and addition are continually stressed throughout.

Children are introduced to standard methods of recording addition and subtraction calculations in the latter part of Year 3, and this is consolidated in Year 4, including calculations of the form HTU $\pm$ HTU. In Year 5, the calculations are extended to include 4-digit numbers, and 1- and 2-place decimal numbers.

Whenever standard methods of addition and subtraction are used for recording, Abacus encourages the children to write an estimated answer before doing the calculation. The estimated and calculated answers can then be compared.

8. Specific guidance on mathematical content

Multiplication and division

At Key Stage 1, the ×2, ×5 and ×10 multiplication tables are introduced. Children are encouraged to read '6 × 2', for example, in different ways as *Six twos, Six lots of two, Six groups of two*, and so on.

In Year 3 the concepts of multiplication and division are consolidated through the arrangement of objects in arrays, from which the commutative property (i.e. 3 × 4 = 4 × 3) is recognised and emphasised. The ×3 and ×4 tables are introduced and mental recall of the associated multiplication and division facts is encouraged.

In Year 4, the mental recall of multiplication and division facts associated with the ×2, ×3, ×4, ×5 and ×10 tables is rehearsed. Children are introduced to the ×6 and ×8 tables, through the concept of doubling the ×3 and ×4 tables. The ×7 and ×9 multiplication tables are also introduced.

In Year 5, children are encouraged to rehearse and develop their ability to mentally recall multiplication and division facts. They should begin to use these to mentally multiply 2- and 3-digit multiples of 10 and 100 by a 1-digit number using the associative law, e.g. 80 × 6 = (8 × 6) × 10.

Throughout Key Stage 2, the 'grouping' concept of division is consolidated, allowing division and multiplication to be developed together. Children are encouraged to read '45 ÷ 5 =', for example, in two ways: *Forty-five divided by five is...?* and *How many fives make forty-five...?*

The concept of a remainder when dividing is established in Year 3, and consolidated in Year 4. In Year 5, children are encouraged to express the remainder as a fraction.

Doubling and halving skills are developed in Year 3 to include the doubles of all numbers up to 20, and doubles of multiples of 5 up to 100. In Years 4 and 5, this is further developed to include doubles of all numbers up to 100, doubles of multiples of 10 up to 1000, and multiples of 100 up to 10 000.

In Year 3 pupils are introduced to the multiplication of 1-digit numbers by both 10 and 100, as well as the multiplication of 2-digit numbers by 10. In Year 4, this is extended to include larger numbers as well as division by 10. In Year 5, larger numbers are multiplied or divided by both 10 and 100. The children are encouraged to view multiplying (or dividing) by 10 or 100, as sliding the digits one or two places to the left (or right).

In the latter stages of Year 4, children are introduced to informal recording methods, and standard written methods for TU × U, and TU ÷ U. In Year 5, this is extended to include HTU × U, TU × TU, U·t × U and HTU ÷ U.

As with addition and subtraction, children are encouraged to make estimates and compare these with their calculated answers.

Money

Abacus uses money to provide a 'real life' and familiar context within which to locate many of the numerical operations and concepts. Children are encouraged to see 'hundreds, tens and units' in terms of pound coins, ten pence pieces and one penny pieces. All children will regard money and coins as both interesting and important. Its use as a structured model for place-value capitalises on this interest.

Children see adults using, enjoying and worrying about money. They are well aware of the importance accorded to money in our society. They know that money transactions are an essential part of our daily lives. Unlike coloured bricks,

8. Specific guidance on mathematical content

blocks or interlocking cubes, money has an importance and a reality outside the primary classroom. It is this fact that makes money such a powerful teaching tool. Children want to operate using money. They want to understand how money works, and to participate in the adult transactions that they see around them.

Measures

In all aspects of measures (e.g. length, weight, capacity, angle), Abacus provides pupils with activities which develop the important skills of estimation. Providing children with estimating experiences enhances their understanding of the measurement concepts involved.

In length, Abacus 5 encourages children to recognise the relationship between millimetres, centimetres, metres and kilometres, and to convert from one unit to another. Use of the relationship between miles and kilometres is also encouraged.

Similarly, the relationships between grams and kilograms in weight, and litres and millilitres in capacity are rehearsed. Pints are introduced as a measure of capacity in Year 4, and gallons in Year 5, when the relationship between pints, gallons and litres is consolidated.

Weight and mass

Throughout this stage of work in Abacus the word 'weight' is used in preference to 'mass'. Scientifically, the weight is the force exerted by the Earth's gravitational field on an object: weight can then be crudely interpreted as the pull towards the ground. The mass of an object is the quantity of matter it contains. The force of attraction varies with the position of the object, but the quantity of matter remains fixed. So, for example, an astronaut weighs less on the Moon because the Moon's gravitational attraction is weaker than the Earth's. The astronaut's mass - the amount of matter in his body – is unchanged.

The weight of an object can be found by using a spring balance, bathroom scale or direct-reading kitchen scale, but the mass has to be found by using balance scales where an object is placed in one pan and a balance obtained by placing objects of known mass in the other.

Later in Abacus, this distinction (rarely made in daily life) will be relatively easy to grasp, but at this stage the word weight is used in accordance with its everyday usage. If you are concerned about this decision, the word mass may be used when it is obviously more appropriate.

Area and perimeter

The concept of area is introduced in Abacus 4 as 'covering' of flat (2-d) surfaces. The square centimetre is introduced as a standard unit. In Abacus 5 the formula for calculating the area of a rectangle is established. Other standard units are introduced, e.g. cm^2, m^2. The meaning of 'perimeter' is introduced in Abacus 4 and developed in Abacus 5 to include calculating the perimeter of a rectangle.

Shapes

'Vertex' replaces 'corner' in Abacus 3. The correct terminology is 'sides' and 'vertices' for 2-d shapes, and 'faces', 'edges' and 'vertices' for 3-d shapes.

Polygons and polyhedra

Children are introduced to the term 'polygon' as a flat (2-d) shape with straight sides. They are then encouraged to distinguish between regular polygons (all sides

8. Specific guidance on mathematical content

the same length, and all angles the same size) and irregular polygons (sides of different lengths, and angles of different sizes). It is important that children see both regular and irregular polygons. Many pentagons, for example, found in packs of 2-d shapes tend to be regular.

The concept of regular polygons leads to the beginnings of classifying triangles. Equilateral and isosceles triangles are introduced in Year 4, right angled and scalene triangles in Year 5.

The distinction between 2- and 3-dimensional shapes is also considered in Abacus 5. In 3-d shape, the term 'polyhedron' is introduced, as a 3-d shape whose faces are all polygons. Children rehearse the concept of a 'net' of a 3-d shape, and how to use one to construct a shape.

Angle

In Year 3, the children's concept of 'direction' is introduced using the four-point directional compass, and this is used to enhance the concept of angle as a measure of turn, using right angles. In Year 4, the eight-point compass is introduced, as well as the 'degree' as a measure of angle. The relationship between degrees and right angles is established.

In Year 5, children are introduced to the protractor as a tool for measuring and drawing angles. The names of types of angle, i.e. acute, obtuse and reflex are also discussed, as are methods for calculating angles, given others, in a right angle and on a straight line.

Position

Position on a grid can be located in two different ways, and it is important to distinguish between them. If the horizontal and vertical lines of the grid are labelled, then positions are located by the point where the two lines meet. If the spaces between the grid lines are labelled, then the positions are located by the grid cell where the two spaces meet.

In Abacus 3 we focus on locating position by labelling the spaces. In Abacus 4, locating position is extended to identifying points (coordinates). This is developed in Abacus 5, introducing terms such as 'origin', 'x-axis' and 'y-axis'.

Graphs

Abacus requires that all graphs are titled and have labelled axes. Usually the horizontal axis represents the item (e.g. types of sport) and the vertical axis represents frequency (e.g. number of votes).

Block graphs are introduced in Abacus 1 and 2, bar graphs in Abacus 3 and 4. In Abacus 5, the bar graph is the basis for introducing bar-line graphs. Line graphs, e.g. temperature graphs are also introduced.

Probability

Probability is introduced for the first time in Abacus 5. Children are required to assess and order events in terms of degrees of likelihood, e.g. 'impossible', 'very likely', and so on.

Framework for teaching mathematics matching chart

Numbers and the number system

Place value, ordering and rounding (whole numbers)

Read and write whole numbers in figures and words, and know what each digit represents.	N1
Multiply and divide any integer up to 10 000 by 10 or 100 and understand the effect.	N15
Use the vocabulary of comparing and ordering numbers, including symbols such as <, >, ≤, ≥, =. Give one or more numbers lying between two given numbers. Order a set of integers less than 1 million.	N1
Use the vocabulary of estimation and approximation. Make and justify estimates of large numbers, and estimate simple proportions such as one third, seven tenths.	Throughout
Round any integer up to 10 000 to the nearest 10, 100 or 1000.	N2
Order a given set of positive and negative integers. Calculate a temperature rise or fall across 0 °C.	N30

Properties of numbers and number sequences

Recognise and extend number sequences formed by counting from any number in steps of constant size, extending beyond zero when counting back.	N13
Make general statements about odd or even numbers, including the outcome of sums and differences.	N42
Recognise multiples of 6, 7, 8 and 9, up to the tenth multiple.	N14
Know and apply tests of divisibility by 2, 4, 5, 10 or 100.	N28
Know squares of numbers to at least 10×10.	N43
Find all the pairs of factors of any number up to 100.	N29

Fractions and decimals

Use fraction notation, including mixed numbers, and the vocabulary numerator and denominator.	N7
Change an improper fraction to a mixed number (e.g. change $\frac{13}{10}$ to $1\frac{3}{10}$).	N7
Recognise when two simple fractions are equivalent including relating hundredths to tenths.	N8
Order a set of fractions such as 2, $2\frac{3}{4}$, $1\frac{3}{4}$, $2\frac{1}{2}$, $1\frac{1}{2}$, and position them on a number line.	N8
Relate fractions to division.	N9
Use division to find simple fractions, including tenths and hundredths, of numbers and quantities (e.g. $\frac{3}{4}$ of 12, $\frac{3}{10}$ of 50, $\frac{3}{100}$ of £3).	N9
Solve simple problems using ideas of ratio and proportion.	Warm-ups
Use decimal notation for tenths and hundredths.	N21
Know what each digit represents in a number with up to two decimal places.	N21
Order a set of numbers or measurements with the same number of decimal places.	N21
Round a number with one or two decimal places to the nearest integer.	N35, N38
Relate fractions to their decimal representations: that is, recognise the equivalence between the decimal and fraction forms of one half, one quarter, three quarters ... and tenths and hundredths (e.g. $\frac{7}{10} = 0.7$, $\frac{27}{100} = 0.27$).	N22
Begin to understand percentage as the number of parts in every 100.	N37, Warm-ups
Find simple percentages of small whole number quantities.	N37
Express one half, one quarter, three quarters, and tenths and hundredths, as percentages (e.g. Know that $\frac{3}{4} = 75\%$).	N37

Framework for teaching mathematics matching chart (cont.)

Calculations

Rapid recall of addition and subtraction facts

Derive quickly or continue to derive quickly: decimals that total 1 (e.g. 0·2 + 0·8) or 10 (6·2 + 3·8); all 2-digit pairs that total 100 (e.g. 43 + 57); all pairs of multiples of 50 with a total of 1000 (e.g. 350 + 650).	N10, N36, N38

Mental calculation strategies (+ and −)

Find differences mentally by counting up through the next multiple of 10, 100, or 1000.	N25, N27
Partition into H, T and U, adding or subtracting the most significant digits first.	N23
Identify near doubles, such as 1·5 + 1·6.	Warm-ups
Develop further the relationship between addition and subtraction.	N40
Add or subtract the nearest multiple of 10 or 100, then adjust.	N24
Add several numbers (e.g. four or five single digits, or multiples of 10 such as 40 + 50 + 80).	N11
Use known number facts and place-value for mental addition and subtraction.	Throughout

Pencil and paper procedures (+ and −)

Use informal pencil and paper methods to support, record or explain additions and subtractions.	N11, N12
Extend written methods to column addition/subtraction of two integers less than 10 000.	N12
Extend written methods to addition of more than two integers less than 10 000.	N12
Extend written methods to addition or subtraction of a pair of decimal fractions, both with one or both with two decimal places (e.g. £29·78 + £53·34).	N39, N41

Understanding multiplication and division

Understand the effect of and the relationships between the four operations, and the principles (not the names) of the arithmetic laws as they apply to multiplication.	N19 and throughout
Begin to use brackets.	N19
Begin to express a quotient as a fraction, or as a decimal when dividing a whole number by 2, 4, 5 or 10, or when dividing £·p.	N4, N15
Round up or down after division, depending on the context.	N4

Rapid recall of multiplication and division facts

Know by heart all multiplication facts up to 10 × 10. Derive quickly or continue to derive quickly: division facts corresponding to tables up to 10 × 10, doubles of all whole numbers 1 to 100, doubles of multiples of 10 to 1000, doubles of multiples of 100 to 10 000 and the corresponding halves.	N3, N5

Mental calculation strategies (× and ÷)

Use doubling or halving, starting from known facts. For example: double/halve any 2-digit number by doubling/halving the tens first; double one number and halve the other; to multiply by 25, multiply by 100 then divide by 4; find the ×16 table facts by doubling the ×8 table; find sixths by halving thirds.	N5, N16, N17
Use factors.	N29
Use closely related facts: multiply by 19 or 21 by multiplying by 20 and adjusting.	N6, N16
Partition and use the distributive law.	N19
Use the relationship between multiplication and division.	N5, N6
Use known number facts and place-value to multiply and divide mentally.	N18 and throughout

Framework for teaching mathematics matching chart (cont.)

Pencil and paper procedures (x and ÷)

Approximate first. Use informal pencil and paper methods to support, record or explain multiplications and divisions.	N31, N33
Extend written methods to short multiplication of HTU by U.	N31
Extend written methods to long multiplication of TU by TU.	N31
Extend written methods to short multiplication of simple decimals with one decimal place.	N32
Extend written methods to short division of HTU by U (with integer remainder).	N33, N34

Using a calculator and checking results of calculations

Develop calculator skills and use a calculator effectively.	N16, N17, N20
Check with the inverse operation when using a calculator.	Encouraged throughout
Check with an equivalent calculation.	N16, N17, N20 and throughout
Estimate by approximating (round to nearest 10 or 100), then check result.	N12, N26, N31, N32 N33, N34, N39, N41
Use knowledge of sums and differences of odd/even numbers.	N42

Solving problems

Making decisions

Choose and use appropriate number operations to solve problems, and appropriate ways of calculating: mental, mental with jottings, written methods, calculator.	Throughout

Reasoning and generalising about numbers or shapes

Explain methods and reasoning, orally and in writing.	Throughout
Solve mathematical problems or puzzles, recognise and explain patterns and relationships, generalise and predict.	Throughout
Suggest extensions asking 'what if ... ?'.	Throughout
Make and investigate a general statement about familiar numbers or shapes by finding examples that satisfy it.	Throughout
Explain a generalised relationship (formula) in words.	Throughout

Problems involving 'real life', money and measures

Use all four operations to solve simple word problems involving numbers and quantities based on 'real life', money and measures (including time), using one or more steps, including making simple conversions of pounds to foreign currency and finding simple percentages.	Warm-ups and throughout
Explain methods and reasoning.	Throughout

Measures, shape and space

Measures

Use, read and write standard metric units (km, m, cm, mm, kg, g, l, ml), including their abbreviations, and relationships between them.	M1, M2, M5
Convert larger to smaller units (e.g. km to m, m to cm or mm to g, l to ml).	M1, M2, M5
Know imperial units (mile, pint, gallon).	M1, M5
Suggest suitable units and measuring equipment to estimate or measure length, mass or capacity.	M1, M2, M5

Framework for Teaching Mathematics matching chart (cont.) — 5

Measures (cont.)

Measure and draw lines to the nearest millimetre.	M1
Record estimates and readings from scales to a suitable degree of accuracy.	M1, M2, M5
Understand area measured in square centimetres (cm^2).	M3
Understand and use the formula in words, length × breadth for the area of a rectangle.	M3
Understand, measure and calculate perimeters of rectangles and regular polygons.	M4
Use units of time.	M6
Read the time on a 24-hour digital clock and use 24-hour clock notation, such as 19:53.	M7
Use timetables.	M7

Shape and space

Recognise properties of rectangles (including diagonal properties) and other polygons.	S2
Classify triangles (isosceles, equilateral, scalene), using criteria such as equal sides, equal angles, lines of symmetry.	S3
Classify solids according to properties such as shapes of faces, number of faces, vertices and edges.	S5
Visualise and draw 3-d shapes from 2-d drawings.	S2
Make shapes with increasing accuracy.	S5
Identify different nets for an open cube.	S5
Recognise reflective symmetry in regular polygons: for example, know that a square has four axes of symmetry and an equilateral triangle has three.	S4
Complete symmetrical patterns with two lines of symmetry at right angles.	S4
Recognise where a shape will be after reflection in a mirror line parallel to one side (sides not all parallel or perpendicular to the mirror line).	S4
Recognise where a shape will be after a translation.	S6, S7
Read and plot coordinates in the first quadrant.	S7
Recognise perpendicular and parallel lines.	S1
Understand and use angle measure in degrees.	S8, S9, S10
Identify, estimate and order acute and obtuse angles.	S9, S10
Use a protractor (angle measurer) to measure acute and obtuse angles to the nearest 5°.	S9, S10
Use a protractor (angle measurer) to draw acute and obtuse angles to the nearest 5°.	S9, S10
Calculate angles in a straight line.	S8
Recognise rotations.	S6
Make patterns by rotating shapes.	S6

Handling data

Organising and interpreting data

Discuss the chance or likelihood of particular events.	D3
Solve a problem by representing and interpreting data in tables, charts, graphs and diagrams, for example: bar-line charts, vertical axis labelled in 2s, 5s, 10s, 20s, or 100s, first where intermediate points have no meaning (e.g. scores on a dice rolled 50 times), then where they may have meaning (e.g. room temperature over time).	D1, D2
Find the mode of a set of data.	D1

10 Classroom materials

Materials provided in the Resource Bank

Number line (0 to 20) – large, double-sided, full-colour number cards, for demonstration
Number line (0 to 100) – medium, double-sided two-colour number cards, for demonstration
Class pack of small number cards (0 to 10) – 30 sets, for individual children
Group pack of small number cards (0 to 10) – 10 sets for group work
Group pack of small number cards (0 to 30) – 5 sets for group work
Pack of small number cards (0 to 100) – 1 set for group work
Wall chart pack (0 to 99 grid and 1 to 100 grid) – 6 sets for a school
Place-value cards (standard pack) – 5 sets of units, tens and hundreds
Place-value cards (extended pack) – 5 sets of units, tens, hundreds, thousands, tenths and hundredths.
Other specialised resources, such as small number grids and number tracks, are included as Photocopy Masters in the Activity Book.

Games Pack

8 games referenced to specific Teacher Card Units.

Assumed mathematical materials in the classroom

Interlocking cubes
Counters
Spotty dice (1 to 6)
Numbered dice (1 to 6) and (1 to 10)
Blank dice
Calculators
Dominoes
Playing cards
Coins (real and plastic)
Base 10 equipment
Sets of plastic 2-d shapes
Sets of solid 3-d shapes
Plastic mirrors
Containers (various, for Capacity)
Measuring jug (100 ml divisions)

Analogue clock with movable hands
Digital clock
10-division counting sticks
Seconds timer or stopclock
Calendar
Weighing balances/weighing scales/ kitchen scales
Set of weights
Rulers/metre sticks/tape measures
Cm-squared paper
Geoboards and rubber bands
Eight-point direction compass
Protractors
Right-angle templates
Graph paper

Other materials

Washing line with pegs attached
Hoops
Cloth (Feely) bags/bean bags
Blu-tack
Pasta shapes/dried beans/lentils
Objects for weighing
Hats
Blank postcards
Train/bus timetables

3-d model-making equipment e.g. Polydron, Clixi, ...
Post-it notes
Plastic spider/fly
Road map
Encyclopedia
TV guide
String
Thermometer

11 Assessment grid (Key Stage 2)

To assist with statutory assessment, selected items from the level descriptions are included within the scheme. For each item, key stages within the scheme are identified. This gives you a quick reference for reporting progress. Each item is presented in the form:

I can...

multiply and divide by 10 and 100.
Abacus 3 N37

You can then quickly assess achievement using an on/off principle. The child **can do** or **cannot do**. There are no interim stages on the records.
- The system allows a cumulative record to develop.
- Each box can be completed in a variety of ways:
  – a simple tick or colouring in by you or pupil;
  – a colouring in using a different colour for each year: red for Reception, blue for Year 1, green for Year 2, ... yellow for Year 6;
  – or preferably a short comment on a particular child's attainment.

At the bottom of each box is a code showing where to check this particular statement (see above).
In some instances this will be at different stages within the scheme to match the development of individual children. Your observations during mental warm-ups, focused group work, or written evidence from Textbooks and Assessment sheets will provide plenty of evidence of achievement for each statement. The record sheets can also be used as: a prompt at the planning stage, part of a record of achievement, a tool for feeding back to parents, a check of a child's individual progress, an assessment of group or whole class progress.

The items included within the assessment grid are taken from the appropriate level descriptions of each attainment target in the National Curriculum. You will be able to use the cumulative information contained within the grid, together with your global view of the child's progress and any other factors you think appropriate, in coming to a decision about whether the child has successfully achieved the appropriate level within each attainment target.

There is no suggestion that the grid alone will provide the only evidence for making end of year or end of key stage assessments. Abacus is in full accord with the objectives in the National Curriculum in wanting these decisions to be based on the level description as a whole rather than simply a collection of disparate items.

Assessment grid: Key Stage 2
Using and applying mathematics

5

Name_____

I can ...

Level 3	Level 4	Level 5
find ways of overcoming difficulties when solving problems.	develop my own strategies for solving problems.	carry through a task by identifying and obtaining information, and checking results.
organise my work and check results.	use my own strategies within mathematics and in practical contexts.	describe situations mathematically using symbols, words and diagrams.
discuss mathematics and explain my thinking.	present information and results in a clear and organised way.	draw my own conclusions.
use and interpret mathematical symbols and diagrams	search for a solution by trying out my own ideas.	explain my reasoning.
understand a general statement and match with examples.		

Assessment grid: Key Stage 2
Number

5

Name_____

I can …

Level 3	Level 4	Level 5
read, write, count and order numbers to 1000. Abacus 2 N34 Abacus 3 N7, N8, N36	multiply and divide by 10 and 100. Abacus 3 N37 Abacus 4 N25 Abacus 5 N15	multiply and divide whole numbers and decimals by 10, 100 and 1000.
understand and use place-value in numbers up to 1000. Abacus 2 N36 Abacus 3 N1, N2	read, write and order numbers including decimals with up to 3 places. Abacus 4 N1, N40, N41 Abacus 5 N1, N21	order, add and subtract negative numbers. Abacus 5 N30
use decimal notation and recognise negative numbers in context. Abacus 4 N35, N41	mentally recall multiplication facts up to 10 × 10 and derive corresponding division facts. Abacus 4 N9, N11, N22, N23, N24 Abacus 5 N3	use all four operations with decimals with up to two places. Abacus 5 N36, N38, N39, N41
use mental recall of addition and subtraction facts to 20. Abacus 2 N31 Abacus 3 N3	add and subtract using standard written methods. Abacus 4 N30, N32, N33 Abacus 5 N12, N26, N39, N41	reduce fractions to their simplest form.
recall the ×2, ×3, ×4, ×5 and ×10 tables, and derive associated division facts. Abacus 2 N12, N13, N25 Abacus 3 N9, N25, N27, N39	multiply and divide using standard written methods. Abacus 4 N37, N38, N39 Abacus 5 N31, N32, N34	multiply and divide any 3-digit by a 2-digit number, without a calculator.
add and subtract 2-digit numbers mentally. Abacus 2 N6, N33 Abacus 3 N31, N32, N33	use simple fractions and percentages to describe proportions of a whole. Abacus 4 N12, N13, N27, N28	calculate fractional and percentage parts. Abacus 5 N9, N37
add and subtract 3-digit numbers using written methods. Abacus 3 N42, N43	use and interpret coordinates in the first quadrant. Abacus 4 S7 Abacus 5 S7	use and interpret coordinates in all four quadrants.
use non-unit fractions and recognise equivalent fractions. Abacus 3 N28, N41	use simple formulae expressed in words. Abacus 5 M4	use simple formulae involving up to two operations.

Assessment grid: Key Stage 2
Shapes, Space and Measures

(5)

Name_____

I can ...

Level 3	Level 4	Level 5
sort and classify 2-d and 3-d shapes using mathematical properties. Abacus 2 S1, S4 Abacus 3 S1, S4, S5	construct simple 3-d models and draw 2-d shapes. Abacus 4 S1, S2, S4 Abacus 5 S1, S2, S3, S5	measure and draw accurately when constructing 3-d models.
recognise line symmetry. Abacus 2 S2 Abacus 3 S6	reflect simple shapes in a mirror line. Abacus 4 S3 Abacus 5 S4	measure and draw angles to the nearest degree. Abacus 5 S9
use non-standard and standard units of length, capacity, weight and time. Abacus 2 M2, M5, M6, M10, M11 Abacus 3 M1 to M8	choose and use appropriate units and instruments for measurement. Abacus 4 M1, M2, M3, M6 Abacus 5 M1, M2, M5, M6	identify all the symmetries of 2-d shapes.
	find perimeters and areas of simple shapes using standard units. Abacus 4 M4, M5 Abacus 5 M3, M4	make sensible estimates of measures in everyday situations.
		understand and use the formula for the area of a rectangle. Abacus 5 M3
		convert between metric units, and between common imperial and metric units.

Assessment grid: Key Stage 2
Handling Data

Name_____

I can …

Level 3	Level 4	Level 5
extract and interpret data from simple tables and lists. Abacus 3 D1, D2	construct a frequency table for discrete data. Abacus 3 D2 Abacus 4 D1 Abacus 5 D1	understand and use the mean, mode and median.
construct and interpret bar charts and pictograms. Abacus 3 D3, D4 Abacus 4 D2, D3	use the mode and range to describe sets of data. Abacus 5 D1	compare two simple distributions.
	group data and represent in appropriate diagrams.	interpret graphs and diagrams, including pie charts.
	construct and interpret simple line graphs. Abacus 5 D2	understand and use the probability scale.
		find and justify the probability of an event.

39

12 Planning

The heart of good teaching is understanding the relationship between **what** is taught and **how** best to teach it. The plan is your way of making this connection explicit. In order to be an effective (even excellent) teacher, it is not necessary to spend hours planning. Indeed, sometimes overplanning can be counter-productive. It is necessary to have:

- **Long term plans**, which enable each teacher to know that the pre-requisite skills and strategies needed for a particular piece of mathematics have been covered in previous years.
- **Medium term plans**, which enable each teacher to pace the content coverage over the course of the year, and also to give the appropriate weightings to each part of the curriculum.
- **Short term plans,** which enable each teacher to know exactly what they are teaching, and how they are teaching it, at the start of the topic.

The National Numeracy Strategy states that it is not necessary for teachers to draw up daily lesson plans, providing that the weekly plan has sufficient structure, content and classroom management information.

Long term planning

Any long term plan is now effectively supplied by the Framework for Teaching Mathematics. This outlines the key objectives (and all the other teaching objectives) for each year of the primary curriculum. In very particular circumstances, such as those pertaining to some Special Schools, it may be necessary to adapt the Framework, but for most schools, it supplies an essential long term plan, which staff can use and become familiar with.

Medium term planning

The medium term plan can also be derived from the Framework for Teaching Mathematics. You can copy the Medium term planning grids from the Framework and use them to construct your own individual medium term plans. Exemplar planning grids, mapping the Abacus Teacher Cards and objectives on to the Framework structure are provided at the end of the book, from page 42.

Because of the flexibility of the Abacus Teacher Cards, it is quite easy for you to alter this order, and to adapt it to suit the needs of your own class. The lesson objectives are clearly stated on each Teacher Card and it is, therefore, simple to postpone a Unit, or to exchange one Unit with another, if so desired.

12. Planning

Using Abacus, the time spent on long term and medium term planning has been cut to an absolute minimum. The exemplar planning grids we provide will ensure that the teaching objectives in the Framework for Teaching Mathematics are covered, and that the order and balance of the topics is preserved.

Short term planning

Given the long and medium term planning, the short term planning becomes a relatively simple task. Each week, you select the appropriate Abacus resources for the Unit(s) to be covered, study the Teacher Card(s) noting the teaching objectives and the resources needed, decide how to balance Units (Teacher Cards) over the week and note the objectives for each day on your weekly plan. You should record the resources to be used, and the ways in which you plan to teach the topics concerned. This information is all clearly outlined on the Teacher Cards.

The format of the weekly plan may vary from school to school, although each school will need to have discussed this and to have agreed a common model. Many schools will choose to use the sample plan outline provided by the Numeracy Strategy training materials. Weekly plans can be brief, but will certainly be more detailed for Monday and Tuesday than for later in the week. Any weekly plan will need to incorporate the following information:

- Clear objectives for the mental/oral section. *[Appropriate Warm-up activity]*
- Clear objectives for the main teaching activity. *[Teacher Card, front]*
- Brief outline of the mental/oral activity. *[Appropriate Warm-up activity]*
- Brief outline of the main teaching activity specifying:
  – the model or image being used to teach this topic
  – the resources needed for the lesson
  – the organisation of the class (whole class, groups, paired work…).
  [All on Teacher Card]
- Indication of the teacher's focus (group, individuals …).
- Outline of any differentiated activities. *[Teacher Card, back]*
- Key vocabulary, including key questions. *[Teacher Card]*
- Learning outcomes. *[Teacher Card, back]*
- Brief outline of possible points for the plenary. *[Teacher Card, back]*

It is therefore no exaggeration to say that all of this information can be obtained from the Abacus materials, in particular the Teacher Card and related resources for each Unit. Teachers will need to study the Abacus resources which accompany each Unit and plan their week's lessons accordingly. The questions of classroom management which need to be noted on the plan can be decided in relation to the activities you select from the Activity Book (or the Games Pack) and also from the Textbook pages, Photocopy Masters, the Simmering Activities, Mental Warm-up Activities and Homework Book.

12. Planning

Once a detailed weekly plan has been drawn up, teachers will not need a lesson plan for each day. It is certainly true that, as the teaching progresses, the weekly plan will need to be modified and more detail added for the end of the week. However, this does not necessitate starting afresh, but rather adapting what has already been outlined.

Summary

The starting point for the weekly plan is the medium term plan, which is drawn from the Framework (exemplars for Abacus are provided at the end of this book). The weekly plan needs to provide clear information about:
- what you are teaching – clear objectives for each part of the lesson each day
- how you are teaching it – outline of the teaching in each part
- how the class is to be managed – any differentiated activities and your focus each day
- what the children have learned and how you will evaluate this.

Once you have a good weekly plan, daily lesson plans are unnecessary.

Within Abacus, all the necessary information to enable you to plan as above is available in a simple and unambiguous form on the Teacher Card for each Unit.

Planning grids

The tables on the following pages show one way of matching the Abacus Units to the Numeracy Framework Planning Grids. They are arranged termly.

You may wish to match the Abacus Units to the Planning Grids in a different order, or you may wish to use your own planning grids. Clearly, whichever order you use, your ongoing evaluation and assessment will inform the development of the scheme of work during the course of the year.

Exemplar planning grid: autumn 5

Unit	Topic	Abacus Unit	Teaching Points	Notes
1	Place value, ordering and rounding Using a calculator	N1 Place-value	To recognise place-value in large numbers To give one more/one less than any whole number up to one million To read, write, order and compare whole numbers using '<', '>' and '=' signs	
		N2 Place-value	To round any number up to 10 000 to the nearest ten, hundred or thousand	
2-3	Understanding × and ÷ Mental calculation strategies (× and ÷)	N3 Multiplication/division	To mentally recall multiplication facts up to 10 × 10 To multiply by zero To mentally derive corresponding division facts	
	Pencil and paper procedures (× and ÷)	N4 Multiplication/division	To rehearse the concept of remainder, when dividing To divide, giving the remainder as a fraction or a decimal To round up or down after division, as appropriate	
	Money and 'real life' problems	N5 Multiplication/division	To double numbers up to 100, and to halve even numbers up to 200 To double multiples of 10 to 1000, and to halve the corresponding doubles To double multiples of 100 up to 10 000, and to halve the corresponding doubles	
	Making decisions and checking results, including using a calculator	N6 Multiplication/division	To recognise the relationship between multiplication and division To recognise that from one multiplication or division fact, three others can be derived	
4-5	Fractions, decimals and percentages Ratio and proportion	N7 Fractions/decimals	To rehearse recognition of fraction notation, including mixed numbers To convert a mixed number into an improper fraction and vice versa To introduce the vocabulary of 'numerator' and 'denominator'	
		N8 Fractions/decimals	To rehearse recognition of equivalent fractions To relate hundredths to tenths	
		N9 Fractions/decimals	To find fractions of quantities To relate fractions to division To recognise simple relationships between fractions	
6	Handling data Using a calculator	D1 Bar-line graphs	To introduce bar-line graphs To draw and interpret a bar-line graph To introduce the 'mode' and 'range' of a set of data	
7	Assess and review			

Exemplar planning grid: autumn (cont.) 5

Unit	Topic	Abacus Unit	Teaching Points	Notes
8-10	Shape and space Reasoning about shapes Measures, including problems	S1 2-d shape	To rehearse the terms 'horizontal' and 'vertical' To introduce the terms 'parallel' and 'perpendicular' To identify parallel and perpendicular lines in polygons	
		S2 2-d shape	To rehearse the names and properties of 2-d shapes To rehearse regular and irregular polygons To introduce diagonals of polygons To introduce the terms 'two-dimensional' and 'three-dimensional'	
		S3 2-d shape	To rehearse recognition of equilateral and isosceles triangles To introduce right-angled and scalene triangles To name and classify different triangles To recognise the properties of different types of triangle	
		S4 Symmetry	To understand the concept of reflection To introduce the terms 'reflective symmetry' and 'axis of symmetry' To recognise lines of symmetry in regular polygons To draw the reflection of shapes in a mirror line	
		M1 Length	To use, read and write standard units of length and convert larger to smaller units, and vice versa To suggest suitable units and tools to measure different lengths To measure and draw lines to the nearest millimetre	
		M2 Weight	To use, read and write standard units of weight and convert larger to smaller units, and vice versa To suggest suitable units and tools to measure different weights To measure the weight of several objects using scales	
11	Mental calculation strategies (+ and −) Pencil and paper procedures (+ and −) Money and 'real life' problems Making decisions and checking results, including using a calculator	N10 Addition/subtraction	To rehearse addition pairs to 100 (multiples of 5) To rehearse addition pairs to 100 (any 2-digit number) To rehearse addition pairs to 1000 (multiples of 50) To recognise what must be added to a 3-digit number to make the next multiple of 100 To recognise the relationship between pairs to 100 and pairs to 1000	
		N11 Addition/subtraction	To add several 1-digit numbers To add several numbers (multiples of 10 or 100) To add several 2-digit numbers	
		N12 Addition/subtraction	To add 4-digit numbers using informal written methods To add 4-digit numbers using standard written methods	
12	Properties of numbers Reasoning about numbers	N13 Properties of number	To count on or back in steps of constant size To construct number sequences To recognise patterns in number sequences	
		N14 Properties of number	To rehearse recognition of the multiples of numbers to 10 To introduce the concept of common multiples	
13	Assess and review			

Exemplar planning grid: spring

Unit	Topic	Abacus Unit	Teaching Points	Notes
1	Place-value, ordering and rounding Using a calculator	N15 Place-value	To multiply and divide any positive integer up to 10 000 by 10 or 100	
2-3	Understanding × and ÷ Mental calculation strategies (× and ÷)	N16 Multiplication/division	To use halving and doubling to help multiply To derive harder multiplication facts by doubling easier facts To multiply two numbers by halving one and doubling the other	
	Pencil and paper procedures (× and ÷) Money and 'real-life' problems	N17 Multiplication/division	To multiply by 5, by multiplying by 10, then halving To multiply by 50, by multiplying by 100, then halving To multiply by 25, using the fact that 4 × 25 = 100	
	Making decisions and checking results, including using a calculator	N18 Multiplication/division	To mentally multiply a 2-digit multiple of 10 by a 1-digit number To mentally multiply a 3-digit multiple of 100 by a 1-digit number To mentally multiply a 3-digit multiple of 100 by a 2-digit multiple of 10	
		N19 Multiplication/division	To rehearse the distributive law for multiplication To multiply mentally by partitioning a number To introduce the use of brackets	
		N20 Multiplication/division	To divide by 4 by halving, then halving again To divide by 8 by halving, halving, and halving again	
4	Fractions, decimals and percentages Using a calculator	N21 Fractions/decimals	To rehearse decimal notation for tenths and hundredths To know the value of each digit in a 2-place decimal number To order a set of decimal numbers	
		N22 Fractions/decimals	To recognise the equivalence between decimals and fractions	
5	Shape and space Reasoning about shapes	S5 3-d shape	To rehearse the names and properties of common 3-d shapes To classify 3-d shapes according to their properties To rehearse 'polyhedron', 'tetrahedron' and introduce 'octahedron'	
		S6 Rotation	To introduce the concept of rotation To recognise the position of shapes after given rotations	
		S7 Position and direction	To rehearse reading and plotting coordinates in the first quadrant To draw and describe polygons based on the coordinates of their vertices	
6	Assess and review			

Exemplar planning grid: spring (cont.)

5

Unit	Topic	Abacus Unit	Teaching Points	Notes
7–8	Measures, including problems Handling data	M3 Area	To understand area measured in square centimetres To understand and use the formula in words, 'length times breadth' for the area of a rectangle	
		M4 Perimeter	To understand, measure and calculate the perimeter of a rectangle To understand, measure and calculate the perimeter of a regular polygon	
		D2 Line graphs	To introduce a line graph To draw and interpret a line graph	
9–10	Mental calculation strategies (+ and –)	N23 Addition/subtraction	To mentally subtract HTU – TU by partitioning To mentally add HTU + TU by partitioning	
	Pencil and paper procedures (+ and –)	N24 Addition/subtraction	To mentally add and subtract near multiples of 10 and of 100	
	Money and 'real-life' problems Making decisions and checking results, including using a calculator	N25 Addition/subtraction	To rehearse the concept of difference and relate it to 'taking away' To find differences mentally by counting up from smaller to larger numbers	
		N26 Addition/subtraction	To subtract ThHTU – HTU using standard written methods	
		N27 Addition/subtraction	To rehearse the concepts of difference and of 'taking away' To make decisions and choose a suitable strategy for a mental subtraction	
11	Properties of numbers Reasoning about numbers	N28 Properties of number	To know and apply tests for divisibility by 2, 4, 5, 10 and 100	
		N29 Properties of number	To introduce the term 'factor' To find all the pairs of factors of any number up to 100	
12	Assess and review			

Exemplar planning grid: summer

Unit	Topic	Abacus Unit	Teaching Points	Notes
1	Place-value, ordering and rounding Using a calculator	N30 Place-value	To rehearse negative numbers by counting back below zero To order a set of positive and negative numbers	
2-3	Understanding × and ÷ Mental calculation strategies (× and ÷)	N31 Multiplication/division	To rehearse multiplying HTU × U using informal written methods To multiply HTU × U and TU × TU using a standard written method	
		N32 Multiplication/division	To multiply U·t × U using a standard written method	
	Pencil and paper procedures (× and ÷)	N33 Multiplication/division	To rehearse the concept of a remainder To rehearse dividing TU ÷ U using informal written methods To divide HTU ÷ U using informal written methods	
	Money and 'real-life' problems Making decisions and checking results, including using a calculator	N34 Multiplication/division	To rehearse dividing TU ÷ U using standard written methods To divide HTU ÷ U using standard written methods	
4-5	Fractions, decimals and percentages Ratio and proportion	N35 Fractions/decimals	To round a 1- or 2-place decimal number to its nearest whole number	
		N36 Fractions/decimals	To mentally add or subtract decimal numbers (crossing units or tenths)	
		N37 Percentages	To introduce a percentage as a fraction of 100 To express simple fractions as percentages To find simple percentages of quantities	
6	Handling data Using a calculator	D3 Probability	To classify events based on degrees of likelihood To recognise the distinction between 'impossible', 'unlikely', 'likely' and 'certain'	
7	Assess and review			

Exemplar planning grid: summer (cont.)

5

Unit	Topic	Abacus Unit	Teaching Points	Notes
8-10	Shape and space Reasoning about shapes Measures, including problems	S8 Angle	To rehearse 'degree' as a measure of angle To rehearse the relationship between degrees and right angles To calculate angles on a straight line	
		S9 Angle	To measure angles using a protractor To draw angles using a protractor To estimate an angle in degrees	
		S10 Angle	To introduce acute, obtuse and reflex angles To recognise acute and obtuse angles in shapes	
		M5 Capacity	To use, read and write standard units of capacity and convert larger to smaller units, and vice versa To suggest suitable units and tools to measure different capacities To measure the capacity of several containers, using a measuring jug	
		M6 Time	To use, read and write units of time and convert larger to smaller units, and vice versa To suggest suitable units and tools to measure different times	
		M7 Time	To use, read and write times using the 24-hour clock To use a timetable	
11	Mental calculation strategies (+ and −) Pencil and paper procedures (+ and −) Money and 'real life' problems Making decisions and checking results, including using a calculator	N38 Addition/subtraction	To recall decimal addition pairs to 1 To recall decimal addition pairs to 10 To recognise what must be added to a decimal number to make the next whole number	
		N39 Addition/subtraction	To add two or more decimal numbers using standard written methods	
		N40 Addition/subtraction	To recognise the relationship between addition and subtraction To recognise that from one addition or subtraction fact, three other related facts can be found	
		N41 Addition/subtraction	To subtract 2-place decimals using standard written methods	
12	Properties of numbers Reasoning about numbers	N42 Properties of number	To rehearse the patterns in the sum of two even/odd numbers To investigate patterns in the differences between two even/odd numbers To explore patterns in the sum of more than two even/odd numbers	
		N43 Properties of number	To introduce square numbers	
13	Assess and review